World Religions

BUDDHISM

Mel Thompson

WALRUS
BOOKS

WORLD RELIGIONS

BUDDHISM   CHRISTIANITY   HINDUISM   ISLAM   JUDAISM   SIKHISM

Visit our website at www.whitecap.ca.

Library and Archives Canada Cataloguing in Publication

Thompson, Mel, 1946-
        Buddhism / Mel Thompson.
(World religions)
Includes index.

ISBN 1-55285-653-4

        1. Buddhism--Juvenile literature.   I. Title. II. Series: World religions (North Vancouver, B.C.)

BQ4032.T46 2005   j294.3   C2004-906002-3

Editorial Manager: Joyce Bentley   Senior Editor: Sarah Nunn
Project Editor: Lionel Bender   Text Editors: Michael March, Peter Harrison
Designer: Richard Johnson   Art Editor: Ben White
Proofreader: Jennifer Smart   Indexer: Peter Harrison
Cover Make-up: Mike Spender, Additional Design
Diagrams and maps: Stefan Chabluk
Picture Researchers: Joanne O'Brien at Circa Photo Library, and Cathy Stastny
Produced by Bender Richardson White, PO Box 266, Uxbridge, UB9 5NX, U.K.

Thanks to Joanne O'Brien at ICOREC, Manchester, U.K. for planning the structure and content of these books.

The Publisher acknowledges the financial support of the Government of Canada through the Book Publishing Industry Development Program for our publishing activities.

Printed and bound in China

Picture Acknowledgments
We wish to thank the following individuals and organizations for their help and assistance, and for supplying material in their collections: Circa Photo Library: pages 5 center, 12, 14, 23, 47, 48–49, 52–53 ; (Rebecca Thompson) 1, 3, 5 top, 19, 22, 25, 26, 28, 36, 38, 54–55; (William Holtby) cover, 5 bottom, 7, 9, 11, 13, 15, 18, 20, 21, 29, 30, 32, 33, 35, 37, 39, 40, 46, 50–51; (John Smith) 44; (T. Halbertsma) 41. Corbis Images: (Tim Page) 27. Lionheart Books: (NASA) 6–7; (BRW) 34. Rebecca Thompson: 4. Topham Photo Library: (Image Works) 8, 16, 17, 42; (Picturepoint)10, 31; (Photri) 43; (Press Association) 45.

CONTENTS

A Buddhist Family

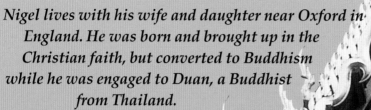

Nigel lives with his wife and daughter near Oxford in England. He was born and brought up in the Christian faith, but converted to Buddhism while he was engaged to Duan, a Buddhist from Thailand.

"**D**UAN AND I have come to visit the Buddhist temple in Wimbledon, south London, with our daughter, Samantha. The temple is built in the style of Buddhist temples found in Thailand.

In the warm sunshine of Thailand, the Eastern architecture of the temple and the orange robes of the monks seem normal, but set against gray English skies here in Oxford, they look unfamiliar. Many who worship at the temple have connections with Thailand; others are Westerners who have chosen to practice Buddhism. Not all these people visit the temple regularly, but they attend the major festivals, to listen to talks given by the monks, and make offerings.

Duan and I have been regular attenders since before Samantha was born. We try to visit the temple once a week. Samantha attends a class for schoolchildren, where she learns not only about Buddhism, but also how to play a Thai musical instrument.

When she was younger, Samantha went to a kindergarten in the temple, where she and other girls and boys would act in plays about the Buddha, the founder of Buddhism. They also drew and painted pictures.

At home we have a small shrine, with statues of the Buddha. Sometimes our family members put flowers on the shrine, leaving them there until they wither, as a reminder that even the most beautiful of things will fade and die. As Buddhists, we try to follow the basic Buddhist teachings on how to live, but, like most Thai Buddhists, we are not vegetarians. In many respects, our family is no different from any other.

At school, Samantha attends religious education lessons and joins in morning prayers. Although she thinks of herself as a Buddhist, she does not mind joining in with other people's religions. To a Buddhist it does not matter how religious you are; what counts is how you live your life. You should not kill, steal, eat too much, tell lies, or get drunk.

Buddhists think that their teachings are mostly common sense."

Buddhists worldwide

The number of Buddhists worldwide is estimated at 360 million, most of whom live in southeast Asia.

ASIA
Most Buddhists live in South Asia, southeast Asia and the Far East. In the East, different countries have different Buddhist traditions. For example, Buddhism in Thailand differs from the Buddhism found in Japan or Tibet.

THE WEST
There are Buddhists all over the world. Some of those in Europe and the U.S.A. have come from traditionally Buddhist countries; others are Westerners who have chosen to follow the Buddhist path.

KINDS OF BUDDHISM
In the west, people can choose from the different kinds of Buddhism, such as Zen, Theravada, or Tibetan Buddhism. They can also join Buddhist groups that try to make Buddhism particularly relevant for Westerners.

What Do Buddhists Believe?

There is no fixed self, Buddhists say. Life depends on other people, and on circumstances over which we have no control. If you were born of the opposite sex, in a different country, to different parents, or if you were very rich or very poor, your life would be different. None of us has a fixed or permanent self, and as our circumstances change, so will we.

THE BUDDHA'S TEACHING is known as *Dharma*. It is the Dharma that helps people see life as it really is. It teaches the Three Universal Truths about life:

1 There is only one thing you can say for sure: everything changes. People are born, they grow old, they die. Places change; rocks wear away, even stars grow old. Nothing lasts forever.

2 Nothing and nobody has a fixed or permanent "self," because everything, including our sense of who we are, depends on everything else. There is no real "you" that is separate from the things that you do, say, or think. Everyone is part of a world in which everything and everyone else is interconnected.

3 Anything may cause you disappointment. Everything changes, you cannot be in total control of your life, and things will not always work out the way you would wish. We all have our limitations. Eventually everyone has to face illness, old age, and death. Even pleasures can disappoint, because they do not last. Human life therefore is inescapably bound up with suffering and disappointment – which Buddhists call *Dukkha*.

Science tells us that everything in the universe is in a state of change: even galaxies are born and die. Belief that everything changes was also the starting point for the Buddha's teaching.

Just as the lotus grows through mud and water to open out into the sunlight, so, Buddhists believe, the human mind can open out and flower. The lotus is a symbol for the awakening mind.

Can we avoid disappointment?

Like a doctor prescribing a cure for an illness, the Buddha set out a way to overcome Dukkha. It is known as the Four Noble Truths:

1 Everything in life may involve disappointment and suffering.
2 Disappointment occurs because we long for things to be different; we want things we cannot have.
3 If we stop wanting the impossible, learn from things that go wrong, and enjoy our life in spite of its limitations, we can achieve happiness.
4 The way to stop craving is to follow the Noble Eightfold Path. This is a series of steps expressing wisdom, practical action, and mental skill.

Open to all

Those who follow the Dharma do not believe it sets them apart from others. They tend not to use labels such as "Christian," or "Buddhist," or "religious," but see Dharma as something that anyone can explore and act on to their own advantage.

Students in a discussion group with their teacher. Buddhists believe that everyone's thoughts and actions are inter-related. We shape our own lives by our karma.

Does everything have a cause?

Everything is the result of an infinite number of causes, Buddhists say. Everything is interconnected, so anything that comes into being does so from causes and conditions. When one thing changes, everything else changes, and when one thing ceases, it affects everything around it. For example, human life could not have evolved on Earth without a breathable atmosphere. That was created by plants, which in their turn developed from cells in water.

Can we change things?

Anything that you think, say, or do will have a result, good or bad, even if you cannot see it immediately. We cannot escape from the pattern of cause and effect. Your deeds affect the lives of others, but they also change your own life, by developing habits. A friendly person tends to be one who looks on the bright side of life; someone who is unfriendly is likely to be negative. You gradually shape your own personality by what you think, say, and do.

Buddha taught that what you are tomorrow depends on what you do today. This is called *karma* (or *kamma*). Your karma are the actions that you choose to carry out. They are like seeds that produce fruit in the future.

Can we know the future?

Buddhists believe that we shape our future by present actions, but we cannot know the future. As we go through life we are shaped by the results of our actions. This is called "re-becoming."

By the time we reach the end of our lives, many of our actions are still like seeds, waiting to produce their fruit. Buddhists believe these actions will influence a life in the future. This future life will not be "you," because Buddhists do not believe in a fixed self, but it will be a life influenced by the results of the one you are living now.

Can we achieve peace?

Buddhists believe that unhappiness is caused by the evils of greed, hatred, and ignorance. Those people who succeed in overcoming these evils will achieve a state of happiness and peace that the Buddhists call *nirvana,* in which they are free from all desire.

Buddhists train the mind to achieve a state of calm. They believe that, through meditation, it is possible to overcome tendencies toward greed and hatred, and to develop insight and compassion toward all other beings.

DEBATE – Can you shape your own life?

Buddhists think that, if you do something good, you will benefit as a result, whether you are acting for yourself or for someone else. If you do something wrong, even if you are never caught, you change yourself a little by your deed, and will suffer the consequences.

So, can you shape your own life?

- No. People are guided from outside by God or by fate.

- Yes. Personal circumstances and choices shape one's life.

How does karma work?

If you are lost and want to find your way, look at a map. Buddhists have the equivalent of a map to show the way that karma affects people's lives. It is called the Wheel of Life.

In the middle of the wheel are three animals: a cock (representing greed), a snake (hatred), and a pig (ignorance). These are shown biting one another's tails, because they feed on one another. Around these there is a circle with

A Tibetan embroidered example of the Wheel of Life, to which everyone is shackled.

people falling downward or floating upward: some lives are improving, others declining. Surrounding these are the six realms:

1　At the top is the world of the gods, and of those who like refined, beautiful things.
2　Moving clockwise, the titans are next. They fight against one another.
3　Then there are the animals, content as long as they have their basic needs.
4　The hell realm of those who suffer comes next.
5　Then there are the "hungry ghosts" – with swords sticking out of their stomachs because they are never satisfied, however much they have.
6　And finally there is the realm of human beings.

These realms represent different ways of living, each with its own problems and opportunities. A Buddha figure appears in each of them, showing people how to improve their lives.

Around the outside of the wheel is a series of images, which shows how karma causes people to move from one realm to another. A blind man, representing ignorance, is followed by a sequence showing how one thing leads on to another. People want things, and the wanting leads on through their own death to a new life being born, only for the whole sequence to start again.

The wheel keeps turning, through life after life, pushed round by greed, hatred, and ignorance. It represents the ordinary world in which we live, which is called *samsara*. It is set within the jaws of a monster, representing death. Buddhists seek to escape from this cycle of behaviour and its consequences. They aim to extinguish the passions caused by greed, hatred, and ignorance, so that they may achieve peace and happiness.

The Wheel of Life

The six realms on the Wheel of Life represent different ways of living. Some people seem like animals, and are easily satisfied. Others are always struggling against one another, or are never content. Each realm has its own opportunities and problems, Buddhists say. But it is possible to move from one realm to another. The human realm is the most fortunate of all, as humans can understand the causes of suffering, and overcome them.

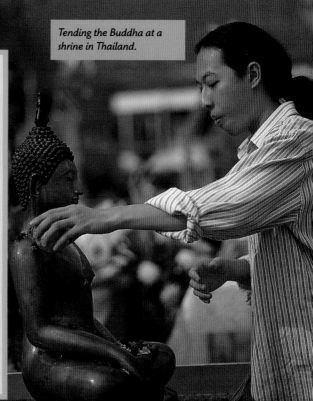

Tending the Buddha at a shrine in Thailand.

How Did Buddhism Start?

The founder of Buddhism was an Indian prince who gave up everything to seek out the truth about life. He found that the biggest problem was suffering, and the way to overcome it was through "enlightenment."

SIDDHARTHA GAUTAMA WAS born in Lumbini, northern India, in 563 B.C.E.. He was the son of a local ruler of the Shakya clan, and is sometimes called Shakyamuni (wise man of the Shakyas). Described as a prince, he grew up in comfort, mixing with the other ruling families. He was trained in the arts, was good at sport, and seemed destined to rule. He married a local princess, Yasodhara, and together they had a son, Rahula.

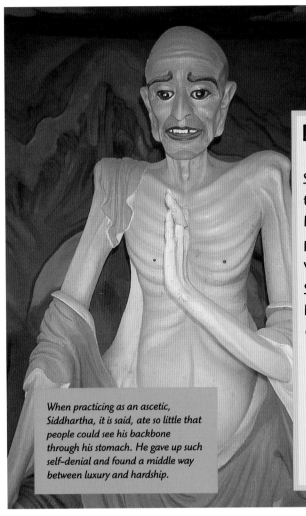

When practicing as an ascetic, Siddhartha, it is said, ate so little that people could see his backbone through his stomach. He gave up such self-denial and found a middle way between luxury and hardship.

DEBATE – Can you be religious at home?

Siddhartha left his home and family to lead a solitary and wandering life, seeking an answer to life's problems. In India at that time, that was not an unusual thing to do.

So, is it possible to be religious at home?

• Yes. Family life offers opportunities to learn the truth about life and religion.

• No. You need to get away from all domestic distractions.

A Buddhist shrine set beneath a pipal tree. Many temples have a bodhi tree (or bo tree) to represent the place where Siddhartha became enlightened.

An answer to suffering?

In India at that time there were many wandering *sadhus* (holy men) who were ascetics. An ascetic is someone who chooses to live simply to gain wisdom. Siddhartha tried this, but gave up after seven years when he felt no nearer to finding the answer to suffering. Determined to discover the truth, he sat beneath a pipal tree and vowed he would not leave that spot until he had found the answer. After a night troubled by temptations, he is said to have become enlightened. The tree under which he sat became known as the bodhi tree, meaning the tree of enlightenment.

At Siddhartha's birth, a seer (wise man, or fortune teller) announced that Siddhartha would grow up to be either a great ruler or religious leader. His parents kept him from witnessing suffering, in the hope that he would not think about humanity's burdens .

One day, he persuaded his charioteer to take him out of the palace into the streets of the city. There he saw four sights that were to change his life: a sick person, an old person, a corpse, and a holy man. Shocked to learn that everyone is liable to sickness, old age, and death, Siddhartha decided that he wanted to leave home and seek an answer to the problem of suffering.

What is enlightenment?

Siddhartha is called "Buddha," which is a title, not a name. It means "the enlightened one." It is impossible to know what enlightenment is like without being enlightened. But the Buddha's teachings about change, and about suffering, and the path to overcome it, were his attempts to explain to people what it was that he came to understand as he sat beneath that tree.

How did the Buddha spread his message?

After his enlightenment, the Buddha went to Sarnath, an ancient holy place. There he met his fellow ascetics, who had deserted him when he gave up his strict discipline. They accepted his new teaching and became his first followers. This is called "the first turning of the wheel of the Dharma."

The Buddha spent the next 40 years traveling around northern India teaching and organizing his followers, who went out to spread his teachings further. In India at that time, wandering teachers were largely supported by householders, who would give them food and shelter, so the Buddha was able to travel and teach. He often stayed just outside a town, so that people would come out to hear him.

What kinds of people followed the Buddha?

A wide variety of people came to the Buddha. Some were householders, who generally came with a particular problem or question. Sometimes he was visited by the wealthy, including those with whom he would have mixed when he lived as a prince. Others were ascetics who, like him, had chosen the homeless, wandering life.

The Buddha always tried to make his teaching relevant to the person he was addressing. He saw no point in debating religious ideas for the sake of it. His aim was to understand and overcome suffering, and his teaching was always directed to that end.

Pilgrims at Sarnath, where the Dharma was first taught, and the Buddhist community (or sangha) was born. Bowing down (or prostration) is a way of showing the Buddha commitment and respect.

In Theravada Buddhist countries it is quite usual for young boys to spend time as novice (or trainee) monks. Few will choose to remain monks later in life.

Who became nuns and monks?

Some of those who followed the Buddha gave up family life in order to travel around and spread his teaching. As time went on, wealthy patrons gave land so that the Buddha could have regular places to rest (called *viharas*.) This was particularly useful during the rainy season, when travel became difficult. Over time, these resting places became teaching centers, where some of his followers began to live. They were the first monasteries, and the full-time followers of Buddha became monks and nuns. They established rules and regulations for living together, recited the Buddha's teachings, and gave advice to those who visited.

DEBATE – Should you accept problems?

The Buddha insisted that people should not run away from life's problems, but look at them clearly and learn from them. When a woman brought him her dead child and asked him to make the child well again, he sent her on a quest to bring him seeds from a house where nobody had ever died. In failing to do so, she learned that death was universal, and so came to terms with her own loss.

So, should you always face the truth?

- No. Truth can be painful. It's sometimes better to dream happily than face the truth.

- Yes. Problems can only be overcome if you face them.

What Is It Like To Be A Buddhist?

In Buddhism there is no god to hand out punishments or rewards. Instead, Buddhists try to create good rather than bad karma. They try to follow general guidelines, called precepts, aiming to produce happiness for themselves and others.

Students enjoy a meal of pizzas containing salami, ham, and beef. Is eating meat a temptation to be avoided, or is it reasonable and healthy to do so? Buddhism offers general principles about lifestyle and habits, but leaves people to decide for themselves.

RELIGIONS THAT TEACH belief in God generally have rules for people to follow. There are rewards for those who keep to the rules, and punishments for those who do not. But because Buddhists see everything as connected with everything else, they do not believe that fixed rules work. What is right for one person might not be right for another. Buddhists do not generally speak about being good or bad, or right or wrong. They speak about being skilful or unskilful. Things are judged skilful if they promote love and acceptance, unskilful if they promote craving, hatred, and ignorance.

The third precept of Buddhism teaches that in a personal relationship, individuals must respect one another's wishes, desires, and feelings: neither partner should be selfish.

What are The Five Precepts?

For most Buddhists, there are just five basic guidelines, called precepts:

1 Not taking life (but trying to cultivate loving kindness toward all creatures)
2 Not stealing (but cultivating open-handed generosity toward all)
3 Not behaving wrongly or selfishly in one's way of life, or being greedy (but trying to develop simplicity and contentment in life)
4 Not lying (but being honest with yourself, as well as with others)
5 Not abusing drink and drugs (but keeping the mind clear).

The five precepts are presented as a guide to the sort of wise and skilful behavior that is likely to lead to happiness. A Buddhist is expected to think about how to apply them to his or her own life, to review how successfully this is being done and to learn from any situations that may have caused suffering or unhappiness. The precepts are a form of spiritual training. Keeping to them is a key part of what it means to be a Buddhist.

On festivals and other special occasions, Buddhists may undertake to follow other precepts as well. Monks and nuns have additional rules and regulations for organizing their lives. They are contained in a special set of writings called the *Vinaya*.

DEBATE - Are rules helpful?

Some religions offer rules and regulations, including food laws. Buddhism offers only general principles, and leaves the decision up to the individual. Some Buddhists are vegetarian; others are not. On the one hand, killing is against the first precept; on the other, people may need meat to stay healthy. Killing an animal yourself is one thing; sharing food offered by a meat-eater is another. So do you need rules?

• Yes. It makes life straightforward; you know when you are doing wrong.

• No. Circumstances change, what is right for one person might be wrong for another.

What is the Noble Eightfold Path?

Siddhartha Gautama had lived both as a wealthy prince and as a poor ascetic. Neither way of life gave him an answer to the world's suffering. He discovered a "middle way" between these extremes, which he set out in the Noble Eightfold Path. The eight steps are not meant to be taken one after another, but are different aspects of the path that Buddhists follow.

The first two are about understanding and attitude (wisdom):

1 Right understanding (of the Buddha's teachings)
2 Right intention (to follow the path).

The next three are about practical ethics:

3 Right speech (to speak in a gentle, not a harsh way; to be positive, not negative or destructive; to be truthful; to speak with a good purpose; not to gossip)

"Western" Buddhists at a countryside retreat in Scotland. Right speech is the precept aimed at promoting honesty and good relationships between people. The Buddha once said that true friendship was the whole of the Buddhist path.

Respecting others

The Buddha saw one of his followers performing a traditional ritual of bowing to the six directions. He explained to his follower that the six directions represent six kinds of human relationships that deserve respect:

- parent and child
- teacher and student
- husband and wife
- friend and friend
- employer and employee
- religious teacher and follower.

Buddhists are therefore encouraged to take seriously the responsibilities that come with each of those relationships, and to respect other people.

4 Right action (keeping the five precepts)
5 Right livelihood (choosing suitable work)

The final three are about meditation and mental training:

6 Right effort (to encourage positive thoughts and remove negative ones)
7 Right mindfulness (to be aware of everything around you)
8 Right contemplation (to practice meditation).

Buddhists are encouraged to balance these three parts. Without wisdom, you cannot see the need for a path. Without mental training, it is difficult to think about the path in a positive way. Without speaking or acting, you cannot put it into practice.

Buddhist worship is all part of following the path. But it is not a separate step, and it does not work by magic. What matter are the intention, the attitude, and the qualities that worship helps to develop in the person who takes part. Worship contributes to both wisdom and mental training.

How do Buddhists find a balanced life?

Some Buddhists think that we all have a Buddha nature within us, and are capable of expressing it. One way of testing progress in this direction is to think about the traditional Buddhist perfections (paramitars), which express the qualities that a Buddha would show. They are generosity, morality, energy, patience, meditation, and wisdom.

Why are there Buddhist monks and nuns?

In the Buddha's time, it was normal for people to leave their ordinary life and spend some time learning from a spiritual teacher. The Buddha's full-time followers started organizing themselves into what became known as the *sangha*. The monks were called *bhikkus*, and the nuns *bhikkunis*. In Theravada and Tibetan Buddhism, it is common for people to enter the monastic sangha, even if for only a short period. When Buddhism arrived in China and Japan, it encountered a culture that was more concerned with family life, so fewer people became monks or nuns.

What does a monk or nun do?

The lives of monks and nuns are based on meditation, study, and work. Each day, there are practical jobs to do in the monastery (vihara), and times for study and meditation. Nuns and monks also gather in the shrine for worship, to express their devotion to the Buddha.

DEBATE - Vows for life?

Christian monks or nuns take vows for life. Buddhists think that this is unrealistic, because circumstances and people are always changing. They therefore take vows for a limited period of time, and can then choose whether to continue in the monastery or go back home. If they decide on the latter, they can always re-enter a monastery. So, should vows be for life?

- Yes. It shows your commitment to your belief in the Dharma.

- No. It is not practical. You may feel differently in the future.

Study is an important part of life for monks and nuns. It deepens their own understanding, and so enables them to teach and advise others.

Nuns and monks take a daily walk into a local village or town, carrying bowls. People come out of their houses, bow to one or other member of the sangha, and place some food in a bowl. The sangha member then bows in return and moves on. This is called the "alms round." Finally, the sangha members return to the monastery to eat what they have been given. It is their main meal of the day, which they take before noon. This may look like begging, but in Buddhist countries it is normal for monks and lay people (those who are not monks or nuns) to help one another. Monks and nuns teach and advise the lay people, and in return the lay people offer them practical gifts, such as food. Giving food to the sangha is also a way of cultivating generosity, so the giver will benefit as well as the sangha that receives the food.

What can monks and nuns own?

Monks and nuns have a limited number of possessions. Apart from their robes, they have a bowl, a needle and cotton, a razor, and a net for straining their drinking water. They also have strings of beads, which they count with their fingers, one bead after another, as an aid to concentration.

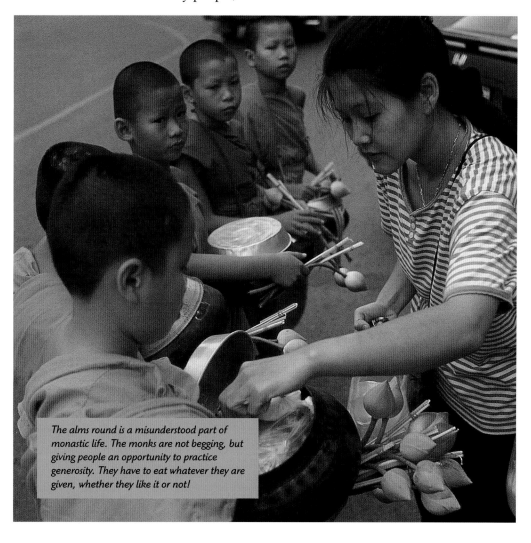

The alms round is a misunderstood part of monastic life. The monks are not begging, but giving people an opportunity to practice generosity. They have to eat whatever they are given, whether they like it or not!

How Do Buddhists Worship?

Many Buddhists think it is helpful to go to a shrine to show respect for the Buddha and to express thanks for his teaching.

UNLIKE OTHER RELIGIONS, Buddhism does not teach belief in a god or gods who have to be worshiped. The Buddha encouraged his followers to think about his teachings, and to accept only those that they understood and found convincing. He taught that people should not put their trust in religious ceremonies, or expect them to work as if by magic. What mattered, he said, was not the ceremonies, but the attitude of the people who took part in them.

How do people become Buddhists?

When they have problems, most people look for a refuge. Faced with the truth about suffering and change, those who follow the Buddha think of themselves

Buddhists use religious ceremonies to express and deepen their own thoughts and feelings. What counts are the inner thoughts, feelings, and intentions of people who enter a temple, not their actions when they are in the temple.

The Pali Canon is arranged in three parts, and is called the Tipitaka, or "three baskets." It includes the teachings of the Buddha, rules for monks and nuns, and philosophical writings.

Buddhism and other religions

Buddhism is not like other religions. It does not insist on people giving up their existing beliefs. When Buddhists went to China, they found two other religions, Confucianism and Taoism. The Buddhists did not try to displace them, but lived alongside them. To this day, many Chinese take part in both Buddhist and other religious ceremonies. Similarly, when Buddhism arrived in the West, it did not require people to set aside all their existing beliefs – it simply suggested that people should not rely too much on religious separation.

as going for refuge to three things: to the Buddha, to his teachings (Dharma), and to his followers (sangha). They believe that these offer a genuine refuge and way of overcoming suffering.

In a simple ceremony, a person declares that he or she intends to go for refuge to the Buddha, the Dharma, and the sangha. This simple act of declaration can be performed as part of a person's regular visit to a shrine or temple for worship (*puja*).

The first time that a person goes for refuge in this way, in the presence of a member of the sangha, is considered the act by which a person becomes a Buddhist. At the same time, the person recites the five precepts that form the basis of the Buddhist way of life.

Do Buddhists read scriptures?

The Buddha did not write his teachings down, but they were passed on by word of mouth for 400 years. The earliest scriptures are the *Pali Canon* (Pali is a language similar to the Buddha's). Later scriptures also claim to be a record of the teachings of the Buddha. One of

the most famous is the *Lotus Sutra*. Buddhist monks and nuns may study the scriptures, but do not look to them to give them answers to all problems. Buddhists try to think things through for themselves. Zen Buddhists believe that the true teaching of the Buddha has been handed down by word of mouth, and so they do not need to read scriptures.

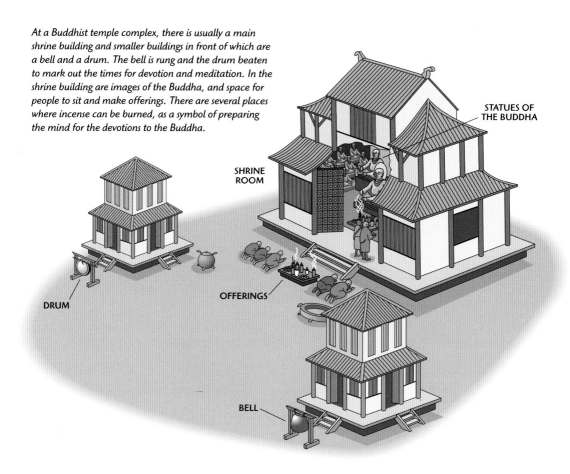

At a Buddhist temple complex, there is usually a main shrine building and smaller buildings in front of which are a bell and a drum. The bell is rung and the drum beaten to mark out the times for devotion and meditation. In the shrine building are images of the Buddha, and space for people to sit and make offerings. There are several places where incense can be burned, as a symbol of preparing the mind for the devotions to the Buddha.

STATUES OF THE BUDDHA

SHRINE ROOM

DRUM

OFFERINGS

BELL

Where do Buddhists worship?

There are a wide variety of monasteries, temples, and shrines in Buddhist countries. A roadside shrine may have just an image of the Buddha, with space for people to place their offerings. Some temples are huge, with many shrine rooms, and different Buddha images. Tibetan temples, in particular, can be very colorful, with large wall-hangings called *thankas*.

Because Buddha is not a god, worship in Buddhist temples is different from worship in other religions. People pay their respects to the Buddha, make offerings, and perhaps sit quietly. There will generally be one or more Buddha images called *rupas*, with candles or lamps burning around them, and space

for offerings of money or flowers. In front of each image, there will usually be a bowl of sand or rice, into which worshipers can put their burning sticks of incense. In front, there is likely to be an open space for people to sit and meditate, chant, or take part in a personal or public ritual. There are often cushions for people to sit on, and in some shrine rooms men sit on one side of the room and women on the other. As well as shrine rooms, a temple will usually have separate rooms, where people can meet with the monks and nuns to discuss problems and get advice.

Why do Buddhist places of worship differ?

As Buddhism spread, its forms of worship became influenced by the cultures within which it was practiced.

The temples in Japan or China differ from those in India or Thailand. The same basic features are found, but the style of decoration is often quite different. When Buddhism arrived in Tibet, it blended with the older religion of the area, called *Bon*, and adopted some of its traditions. Consequently, Tibetan Buddhist shrines are very colorful and their images strange to Western eyes. By contrast, the Zen tradition in Japan seeks to promote calm meditation and everything is kept very simple.

DEBATE - Elaborate or simple?

Some people love elaborate costumes, images, and glimmering candles. Some forms of Buddhism offer this, in the belief that it enables people to engage their emotions and intuition, as well as their mind, in worship. In other forms, it is thought to be more important to help the mind to become still and alert, and that this can best be achieved by sitting in quiet meditation, in simple surroundings that induce calm.

So, are elaborate rituals helpful?

- Yes. They feed the imagination and people can feel involved in worship.

- No. The mind must be clear, with as few distractions as possible.

The simplest form of Buddhist shrine. It consists of an image with space in front where offerings and sticks of incense may be placed.

The Buddha is not worshiped as a god, so much as a great teacher whose wisdom points the way to personal contentment – nirvana.

Do Buddhists worship at home?

Many Buddhists have a small shrine at home. It may consist of one or more Buddha images (rupas), with perhaps a bowl for incense sticks, candles, and some flowers. Tibetan Buddhists in particular like to have a photo of their personal teacher, and this too may be placed on the shrine.

Some Buddhists sit in meditation before their shrine. Others may chant or simply make offerings, and put their hands together as a mark of respect for the Buddha. As with other aspects of Buddhism, there are no rules and regulations about the use of shrines at home. People do whatever they find most helpful.

What traditional offerings are made?

It is traditional for Buddhists to make three offerings before an image of the Buddha. Each of them has a special meaning:

1 A candle or lamp – This represents the light of wisdom, overcoming the darkness of ignorance.
2 A flower – Flowers are beautiful, but quickly fade. They are a reminder that everything in life changes.
3 Incense – It is very common to see people lighting sticks of incense and offering them at a shrine. Just as the smell of the incense spreads out in all directions, so Buddhists hope that the benefit of good deeds will spread outward from the person who performs them.

How do Buddhists gain from worship?

If the Buddha taught that people should not rely on religious ceremonies, why do Buddhists perform *puja*?

People who go to a shrine and make offerings are reminding themselves of the value of following the Buddhist path, and of the qualities that are likely to help them to do so. The person who worships may also feel more calm and focused as a result of the action. However simple the act of devotion, its benefit comes from the inner thoughts and intentions of the person performing it, not from the act itself.

Flowers and human beings, like everything else, change over time. They come into being, blossom, and eventually die. Here, Buddhists offer flowers at a shrine as an expression of this belief.

Finding the path

Not to do evil,
To cultivate what is wholesome,
To purify one's mind:
This is the teaching of the Buddha

From the *Dhammapada*, an early Buddhist scripture

For many Buddhists, trying to follow the five moral precepts is their main task. Others would argue that you cannot do so unless you first calm and direct your mind through meditation. Yet others might say that first you need devotion to the Buddha, to give you the conviction and determination to follow the Buddhist path.

Making a simple offering before an image of the Buddha can be an alternative to sitting for hours in meditation. It helps to direct the mind and expresses a person's values.

Why do Buddhists meditate?

Buddhists believe that, in order to see things as they really are, you need to have a calm and clear mind. Most of the time, our minds rush from one thing to another. We may not be aware of what is happening around us, because we are too busy planning the future or remembering the past. The starting point for meditation is an awareness of your present surroundings, your feelings, and the thoughts that are in your mind. This is the seventh step of the Noble Eightfold Path.

How do Buddhists meditate?

Most forms of meditation are done sitting down, in a comfortable but upright position, to help alertness. Some Buddhists practice a walking meditation, very deliberately taking one step after another, aware of all the sensations of walking and of the ground beneath their feet. There are two basic forms of meditation, called *samatha* and *vipassana*.

Samatha meditation helps the mind to become calm and to focus on one thing at a time. One common form is the mindfulness of breathing. The person becomes aware of the breath entering and leaving the body, and starts by counting breaths in and out. Gradually, he or she is able to be very still and gently aware of the passage of air in and out of the nostrils. This can produce a state of feeling very alert, yet very calm at the same time. Zen meditation involves sitting with your eyes just slightly open, silently facing a wall. If the mind fills with a rush of images and thoughts, the meditator gently sets them to the one side.

Vipassana meditation helps people to gain insight. A Buddhist may meditate on the fact of change, perhaps by looking calmly at some flowers that are growing old and faded, or even on death. At one time, it was customary for monks to sit and meditate on the stages of decomposition of a corpse! The aim of vipassana is to help a person become fully aware of the reality of life exactly as it is, unclouded by prejudices or dreams.

Whether or not to meditate

In the West, many people who practice Buddhism find meditation helpful, and some attend classes in meditation even if they are not Buddhists. In some traditional Buddhist countries, people often think that meditation is difficult and best left to the monks. Meditation helps a person to understand his or her mind, and the way it works. It does not fill the mind with new ideas, and it is not a form of brainwashing. Some might argue that action is more important. Buddhists might reply that action needs to have direction, and that a calm mind helps to achieve this aim.

People sitting silently, in the traditional lotus pose, in a meditation hall. A bell will be rung to mark the different stages in their meditation. Sitting correctly and breathing gently both help to calm the mind.

What Are The Main Kinds Of Buddhism?

As Buddhism spread eastward to southeast Asia, northward to China and Japan, and up into the Himalayan countries of Tibet and Nepal, it adapted itself to the needs of the people and cultures in each of those areas.

THERE ARE THREE main branches, or *yanas*, meaning "vehicles," of Buddhism. They are: Theravada Buddhism, which developed in India and Southeast Asia; Mahayana Buddhism, which developed in China and Japan; and Vajrayana Buddhism, which developed in northern India and Tibet. All three kinds of Buddhism are now found throughout the world. Some modern Buddhist groups blend teachings and practices from all of these traditional forms.

In Theravada Buddhism monks and lay people help one another. Here, in Sri Lanka, at an open-air Buddhist meeting, monks and lay people exchange ideas and thoughts.

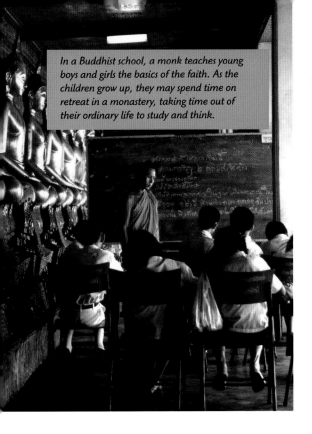

In a Buddhist school, a monk teaches young boys and girls the basics of the faith. As the children grow up, they may spend time on retreat in a monastery, taking time out of their ordinary life to study and think.

What is Theravada Buddhism?

The oldest of the three branches of Buddhism, Theravada Buddhism is probably the closest to the lifestyle and teachings of the historical Buddha. It was originally called the Hinayana, or "small vehicle," because it was seen as a religion mainly for monks, and narrow in its discipline. Theravada means "tradition of the elders."

Monastic life is very important in this tradition. Monks often run schools, so children become used to the idea of being a monk or a nun. Many spend some time in a monastery as a mark of becoming grown-up, and able to take responsibility for their own life and religion. Monks and nuns provide not just education, but advice and help for all who ask for it. On some occasions, when they see that society is unfair, the monks may become active politically and campaign for change. This

happened, for example, in Myanmar (previously Burma) in the latter part of the twentieth century. The monks protested and argued for change, using non-violent methods.

What are Theravada scriptures?

The oldest collection of Buddhist scriptures, the Pali Canon, is used by Theravada Buddhists. Each chapter of the first part of these is called a Sutra. This often starts with the words, "Thus have I heard…" and then gives an account of what the Buddha said on a particular occasion when something happened, or someone came to him with a particular question.

What is Mahayana Buddhism like?

Buddhism has never tried to impose a particular style of life, but rather to help people discover their own way to put its teachings into practice. When Buddhists arrived in China, they found a society with a strong tradition of family life. There were no homeless religious wanderers, as there were in India in the days of the Buddha. Chinese Buddhism became less concerned with monastic life and more family-based. The religions of Confucianism and Taoism already existed in China, and many people were happy to follow all three religions, without having to choose between them. Far Eastern Buddhism is called Mahayana, meaning "large vehicle," because it claims that it is suitable for everyone.

Why is devotion to Amida so popular?

Of all the different Buddha images, Amida (or Amitabha) is very popular in the Far East. This Buddha sits in calm meditation, wearing simple robes. Amida is seen as the Buddha of infinite light. There is a tradition that people who call on Amida will, after this life, go to a paradise where conditions are just right to practice the Dharma. Some Buddhists chant the name of Amida as a form of meditation.

What is Zen?

Meditation has always been important for Buddhists. Zen is the Japanese word for meditation, so Zen Buddhism is based on control of the mind. Zen Buddhists practice sitting and walking meditation, and also test out their minds with impossible questions, called *koans*.

Zen Buddhists also express the simplicity of meditation through the arts. Temples may have gardens of carefully raked sand, and precisely placed rocks and bushes. Zen has inspired painting, calligraphy (decorative writing), and many other activities. It requires a calm waiting for exactly the right moment to do something, or understanding exactly the right line to draw or paint. Zen is based on teachings that are passed on from master to student, and does not rely on scriptures, or other written traditions.

Monks stand in rows to chant in this temple in China. Chanting is an alternative to meditation. A familiar phrase repeated over and over again is meant to create a sense of calm and reinforce a positive attitude of mind.

DEBATE – Does devotion bring nirvana?

In the earliest forms of Buddhism, people did not expect to benefit from religious actions, but from their intentions and behavior. However, some Mahayana Buddhists think Amida Buddha will help them to achieve nirvana if they are devoted to him. They claim devotion shapes their lives. So, does devotion to Amida help?

● Yes. Devotion enables you to enter paradise.

● No. All progress depends on actions and intentions. There are no short cuts.

Two teenagers take refuge through prayer, silence, and meditation at Sule Pagoda in Yangon, Burma.

Tibetan Buddhists worship using prayer wheels. Small pieces of paper with mantras (words to be repeated) written on them are then tucked into the wheel. The wheel is swung round on a handle, or turned by the wind or water. Prayer wheels are a reminder that the Dharma works everywhere and through everything.

What is Tibetan Buddhism?

Buddhism reached Tibet, high in the Himalayas, in about 700 CE, 1 200 years after its beginning. By this time, in northern India, new forms of Buddhism had developed, including Vajrayana, which Buddhist teachers brought to Tibet. "Vajra" in Vajrayana has two meanings: diamond and thunderbolt. Vajrayana is a form of Buddhism that uses many different methods to help people to achieve enlightenment.

Tibetan Buddhism is colorful and noisy, as people engage their emotions as well as their minds. Processions, dancing, and chanting are common at Tibetan festivals. Monks perform a sequence of gestures, called *mudras*, each with its own special significance. Tibetan monks can be distinguished from their southern counterparts by the color of their robes, which are deep red rather than yellow.

How did Tibetan Buddhism spread west?

Until the 1950s, Tibet was a very religious country, largely cut off from the rest of the world, and ruled by the Dalai Lama and the monks. Then the Chinese invaded and claimed Tibet as part of China. They tried to put an end to Buddhism in Tibet, despite opposition from the Tibetan people. The Dalai Lama fled, and became one of a growing number of exiles living in India. Other senior lamas have also escaped, along with many ordinary Buddhists who want to be free to practice their religion. Consequently, many Tibetan teachers now live in Europe and in the U.S.A. They have taught Tibetan Buddhism to Westerners, and it is now known and practiced worldwide.

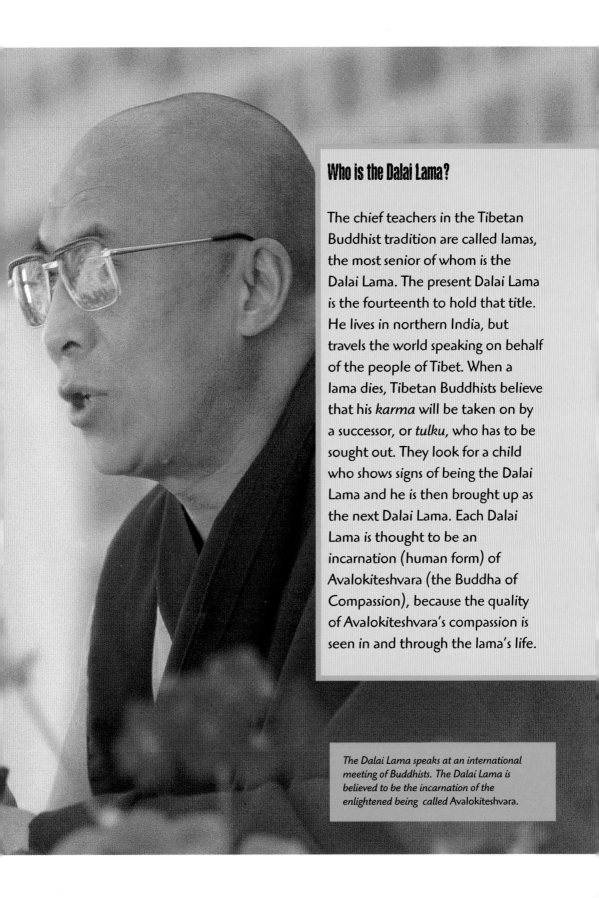

Who is the Dalai Lama?

The chief teachers in the Tibetan Buddhist tradition are called lamas, the most senior of whom is the Dalai Lama. The present Dalai Lama is the fourteenth to hold that title. He lives in northern India, but travels the world speaking on behalf of the people of Tibet. When a lama dies, Tibetan Buddhists believe that his *karma* will be taken on by a successor, or *tulku*, who has to be sought out. They look for a child who shows signs of being the Dalai Lama and he is then brought up as the next Dalai Lama. Each Dalai Lama is thought to be an incarnation (human form) of Avalokiteshvara (the Buddha of Compassion), because the quality of Avalokiteshvara's compassion is seen in and through the lama's life.

The Dalai Lama speaks at an international meeting of Buddhists. The Dalai Lama is believed to be the incarnation of the enlightened being called Avalokiteshvara.

What Do Buddhists Celebrate?

Buddhists have no universally agreed ways of marking the big moments in life – birth, coming of age, marriage, and death. Each country where Buddhism is practiced has developed its own traditions.

IN THERAVADA COUNTRIES, it is usual for Buddhists to marry at a civil ceremony, although they may invite monks to their home to give them a blessing. In Mahayana Buddhism, some temples are registered as places for marriage, and Buddhist monks conduct weddings. Buddhists see marriage as a personal agreement between the partners. If a relationship breaks down, they accept divorce.

When a Buddhist dies, relatives and friends sometimes sit with the body and meditate on the fact of death, and on the qualities of the deceased person.

Buddhist boys become used to monastic life whether as a result of school or by doing a "rains retreat."

Buddhists who die are usually cremated, and their ashes put in a monument called a *stupa*. Some stupas, such as those that are claimed to house remains of the Buddha, are huge. Others are small, often made of wood, and can be placed on or near a shrine.

When a Buddhist teacher dies, particularly in the Tibetan tradition, the ashes may be divided between several stupas, each of which is sent to a monastery, or center, where that teacher had taught.

How do Buddhists mark coming of age?

As a sign of growing up, boys may spend some time in a monastery, living as a monk. Traditionally, this takes place during the rainy season retreat. A boy may first be dressed as a young prince (like Siddhartha), before having his head shaved and putting on monastic robes. Living as a monk for a short time is intended to give young people a sense of discipline. It is a sign that they are now old enough to accept responsibility for themselves. Most of them are happy to return to their ordinary lives after a few weeks.

Can Buddhists be organ donors?

Some Buddhists believe that a new life begins as soon as the person dies. They are therefore happy to allow body organs to be removed for the benefit of other people. Other Buddhists (particularly in the Tibetan tradition) think that a person lingers around his or her old body for some time after death, and removing the organs would disturb the lingering spirit.

An elaborate funeral pyre in Thailand, prepared for the cremation of the mother of a senior monk.

How do Buddhists celebrate New Year?

In Thailand and Burma, New Year is celebrated at the beginning of spring, in April. Water is often used as a symbol of new life. Streams and ponds may dry up in the hot weather, so Buddhists rescue fish and set them free into the rivers. Others free caged birds as a sign of new life. Buddha images are decorated and washed. In Thailand it is quite usual for people to celebrate by having water-fights in the street!

New Year is also a time for celebrating and feasting with families. The festival generally lasts three days. On the third day, people go to the temple to take the "refuges and precepts" as a way of reaffirming their commitment to the Buddha, to his teaching, and to the Buddhist community.

What is Vassa?

In the early days of Buddhism, the Buddha's followers would go out and

One of the traditional ways of celebrating is to eat together. Lay Buddhists sometimes provide food for the monks at festival times, or to mark some important event in the life of their family.

Releasing an eel into fresh water is a way of showing compassion toward all living things – part of the Thai celebration of New Year.

about to teach the Dharma. But the rainy season made traveling difficult, so they stayed behind in their resting places to spend time in meditation and study until it was over. This became known as the *rains retreat*.

The tradition continues to this day. Monks and nuns (particularly in the Theravada tradition) usually spend some time each year in retreat. *Vassa* is the celebration that marks the beginning of the rains retreat. It is the time when young men enter the monastic life for a short period.
The end of the rainy season is marked by a festival called *Kathina*. Then, lay Buddhists come and present gifts to the monks, to help them live through another year. These gifts might be robes, food, or things for use in the monastery.

Celebrating the Buddha's life

Wesak, the festival that celebrates the birth, enlightenment and death of the Buddha is held in April or May. It is the most important festival in Theravada Buddhism. Light is a symbol of enlightenment, so the celebrations include lights and processions with lanterns. People share food and gather to hear talks from the monks. Some Buddhists take extra vows for the day to gain extra merit. It is a time for generosity, and in some parts of the Buddhist world, blood donor sessions are held in temple grounds as an example of this.

What is the O-bon festival?

The Buddhist Wheel of Life includes the realm of the "hungry ghosts," or spirits. Can a hungry spirit be fed, so that it no longer suffers from the pangs of longing? In Japanese Buddhism there is a tradition that, if you feed the monks at the end of a rains retreat, you can save a "hungry spirit," and release it from the realm where it is trapped.

The O-bon festival, which is held in July, originated from this tradition. Candles and lamps are lit to welcome those who have died. For Japanese Buddhists it is a special family holiday, when families remember their ancestors, and especially those who died recently. People often go home to their families for the festival. They may visit the places where their dead relatives lived, or where they died or were cremated. Buddhist priests are invited into the home to recite from the scriptures, and offerings are made at the shrine in the home.

Tibetan monks creating a mandala out of grains of colored sand. The mandala represents the universe. Disposing of the sands is a symbolic action, showing that nothing is permanent.

How do Tibetan Buddhists celebrate?

As well as celebrating the major Buddhist festivals, Tibetan Buddhists celebrate the birthdays of their major teachers. Sometimes, to prepare a temple for a festival, they put up huge wall hangings (*thankas*) on the outside temple walls for all to see. (Usually, thankas are found on the inner walls of temples and shrines.) They may make huge Buddha sculptures out of butter. As the butter melts away, it is a reminder that everything changes.

Buddhist monks may create circular patterns, called *mandalas*, out of colored sands. After all the work, the sand is thrown away, and often tipped into a stream. The lesson here is that one should be prepared to create something beautiful and then let it go. The value is in the making, not in trying to hold on to the finished product.

Tibetan festivals include processions of people in colorful costumes, accompanied by the blowing of horns. The celebrations often use dance and drama to help express different aspects of Buddhist teaching.

This lively procession is part of the celebrations for the opening of a Buddhist monastery in Mongolia. Mongolian Buddhists follow the Vajrayana tradition.

Different traditions, similar aims

There are many forms of Buddhism, from the orderly life of monks in southeast Asia to the simplicity of Zen. Different Buddhist groups accept each other's traditions, because different practices suit different people. The general principle is that, whatever helps to overcome greed, hatred, and ignorance, and to develop wisdom and compassion, is right for that person.

What Has Buddhism To Say About The World Today?

Buddhism has gained widespread appeal from East to West because it addresses many of the issues that face people in the world today – from war and peace, to hunger and health, and alcohol and drug abuse.

Rescue workers pick their way through the remains of the World Trade Center in New York, destroyed by terrorists in 2001. Buddhists oppose all violence and killing, because both violate the First Precept, and they point out that hatred is one of the three poisons that keep people trapped in the cycle of suffering.

Can Buddhists approve of killing?

Not taking life is the first and most basic of the Buddhist precepts. Buddhists seek to avoid killing of any sort, but especially the killing of other people. One Japanese Buddhist group, horrified by the death and suffering on both sides caused by the Second World War, and by the atomic bombs dropped on Hiroshima and Nagasaki, is dedicated to bringing about world peace. The group is called Nipponzan Myohoji, and

Taking recreational drugs runs counter to Buddhist teaching because drugs of this kind cloud the mind.

DEBATE – Should you be vegetarian?

Most Buddhists say that it is ideal to be vegetarian, because it avoids killing animals for food. But some people are told they need to include animal protein in their diet or they may be in danger of making themselves ill. The Dalai Lama, for example, was told he should give up his strictly vegetarian diet. He now eats meat for some of the time. Other people cannot grow enough food to stay alive, and without killing animals they would starve.

So, should you eat animal flesh to stay healthy?

- No. You should always refuse to take life, even if you suffer as a result.

- Yes. Because starving or becoming ill is just as destructive as killing animals.

What about drugs?

The last of the five Buddhist precepts is about keeping the mind clear and not clouding it with drink or drugs. People under the influence of drugs are not fully aware of the world around them, and may behave foolishly. The same is true of someone who is drunk.

Buddhists do not say that alcohol or drugs are wrong in themselves – after all, drugs are an important part of medical treatment. Rather, it is the abuse of these things, in a deliberate attempt to cloud the mind, that is seen as unskilful. To a Buddhist, trying to escape from reality through drugs is impossible, and can only lead to more suffering. Other things too can drug the mind, such as an

throughout the world its members build peace pagodas to symbolize Buddhism's quest for peace.

obsession with computer games or some other activity. Anything that takes over your life so that you can scarcely think about other matters would count as a drug. So even something that is perfectly legal would, under such circumstances, be thought of as "unskilful."

What is your ambition?

Everyone has some particular goal or ambition. Young people, in particular, often identify with stars of the music world or sporting heroes. They may aspire to be rich and lead a celebrity lifestyle like their idols. Buddhism offers an alternative set of images.

Buddhism recognizes that no two people are alike. These differences are illustrated in the variety of images found in Buddhist shrines and temples. Many of them depict *Bodhisattvas* (enlightened beings), each of whom expresses a particular quality. For example, the Bodhisattva Manjushri represents wisdom. He is shown as a prince, wielding the sword of wisdom in one

hand, and holding a book in the other. Students at school or college wishing to clear their thoughts to solve a problem may turn to him for inspiration. Other people might have a need to develop a sense of generosity, or determination. For each of these qualities, there is a particular Buddha image.

If you want to be a great musician, you need to listen to music and watch performers. You see them, and imagine yourself playing or singing in the same way. They inspire you to try to be like them. Similarly, Buddhists meditate on one or other of the Buddha images to develop a particular quality. This is not seen as a selfish ambition, because selfishness is a hindrance to progress,

Outdoor pursuits can be excellent opportunities to develop such qualities as patience, calmness, and care of the environment.

Many youngsters aspire to be rich and famous. It is good to have ambitions, but these should be tempered with a sense of wellbeing and realism.

Choosing a career

In choosing a career, Buddhists try to follow the principle of "right livelihood," the fifth step of the Noble Eightfold Path. This means that work should not require you to break the Buddhist precepts. For example, it would be difficult for a Buddhist to work as a soldier, butcher, or wine merchant, or in any business whose sole aim is to make huge profits. Any work that involves deception, or the exploitation of people for profit, would also involve breaking the precepts. On the other hand, helping the poor, teaching, or providing for people's needs can give a Buddhist opportunities to develop positive qualities. Work is then part of the Buddhist path.

and the very opposite of what the images express. Different people have different ambitions, so there is no one Buddha image that expresses everything that a person can become. Buddhists choose the one that best suits how they see themselves and their lives.

Are men and women equal?

In the Buddha's day, while men sometimes left home to follow the spiritual path as a wandering holy man, women were expected to stay at home and care for a family. But the Buddha said that men and women were equally capable of following the Buddhist path, and of becoming enlightened. Women, he said, could become *anagarikas* (homeless ones) or *bhikkunis* (nuns).

What about abortion and contraception?

Buddhists believe that from the moment a child is conceived it has consciousness in some form, which it receives from earlier lives. They also see human life as a precious opportunity. For these reasons, Buddhists regard abortion as a very serious matter, as it goes against the first precept. For many Buddhists, abortion is only right if the life of the mother is in danger. But contraception is generally welcomed, because over-population can lead to poverty and suffering.

What about the environment?

Buddha taught that everything arises because of causes and conditions: that nothing can exist independently of anything else; that everything is connected with everything else. This was a remarkably scientific way of looking at things for its time, considering that it was put forward some 2 500 years ago.

Thus, Buddhists see human beings as part of a single, ever-changing stream of life, of which the environment is also part. Within this environment, they seek

The world conference on religion and the environment, held in Thailand. It was organized by Buddhists and included representatives of many world religions. Wildlife conservation, pollution, and related environmental issues were discussed.

Human error and accidents can cause disaster to the natural environment. Oil can kill sea birds, and ruin beaches and coastal habitats. Buddhists recognize that we have a responsibility toward all other species and our environment.

to show compassion to all other creatures. Following the law of karma, harm done to the environment is also harm done to oneself.

Is Buddhism scientific?

Scientific thought is based on making observations, testing them out, and trying to find theories to explain them. It does not depend on authority or tradition, but on reason and experience. In this sense, Buddhism is scientific because the Buddha invited people to explore his teachings, to try them out, and to accept them only if they found through their experience that they were true.

DEBATE – Should women become nuns?

Buddha argued that women should be able to become nuns. This was controversial because, at the time, most people expected women to stay at home and bring up a family. So, should a woman leave home and live as a nun?

- Yes. If a man can do it, then so should a woman, if she wants to.
- No. Women are better suited to having children and bringing up a family.

REFERENCE

Buddhism started in India and spread to southeast Asia, northward to China and Japan, and across the Himalayas into Tibet. In modern times it has spread throughout the world, sometimes carried by Buddhists who have decided to emigrate, and also because people from other cultures have chosen to practice Buddhism.

Most Buddhists still live in the traditional Buddhist countries of India, southeast Asia, and the Far East. It spread only gradually, and people were free to follow some of their traditional religious ceremonies alongside the new Buddhist ideas. Each form of Buddhism developed to suit the society of that part of the world.

Theravada Buddhism

Mahayana Buddhism (Tibetan)

Mahayana Buddhism (Chinese-Japanese)

Timeline of Buddhism

563–483 B.C.E. Siddhartha Gautama (the Buddha)
480 B.C.E. First council of monks meets to recite Buddha's teachings
380 B.C.E. Second council of monks agrees the rules for monastic life
273 B.C.E. The Emperor Asoka, ruler of much of India, becomes a Buddhist
c.250 B.C.E. A third council of monks agrees the scriptures to be included
   in the Pali Canon
240 B.C.E. Asoka's son, Mahinda, takes Buddhism to Sri Lanka
1st century B.C.E. First written scriptures (The Pali Canon)
4th century CE Buddhism spreads through China to Korea
6th century Buddhism introduced into Japan
6th century Zen develops from teachings of the Indian monk Bodhidharma
7th century Buddhism introduced into Tibet
12th century Buddhism in India wiped out, mainly through persecution
   by Muslim invaders
17th century Dalai Lamas rule Tibet
20th century   Buddhism spreads to the Western world
1951 Chinese invade Tibet
1959 Dalai Lama escapes to India

Calendar and Major Festivals of Buddhism

Buddhists follow the Dharma in many different ways, and religious ceremonies are optional for them. However, most Buddhists take part in festivals during the year to celebrate particular events and traditions. In particular, festivals offer a chance for them to gather to hear talks on the teachings of the Buddha, to take part in worship, and to strengthen their commitment to the Buddhist way of life. The most important festival of the year is Wesak, which is celebrated by a majority of Buddhists.

New Year (April in Burma and Thailand; January in Japan)
Wesak – birth, enlightenment, and death of the Buddha (April/May)
O-bon – for the "hungry ghosts" (in Japan) July
Asala – first preaching of the Buddha (July/August)
Vassa – start of the "rains" retreat (follows Asala)
Kathina – end of the "rains" retreat (October/November)
(Festivals and dates vary between the three main branches of Buddhism. There are a large number of lesser festivals, especially within Tibetan Buddhism.)

The Six Major Faiths

BUDDHISM
Founded
535 B.C.E. in Northern India

Number of followers
Estimated at 360 million

Holy Places
Bodh Gaya, Sarnath, both in northern India

Holy Books
Tripitaka

Holy Symbol
Eight-spoked wheel

JUDAISM
Founded
In what is now Israel, around 2000 B.C.E.

Number of followers
Around 13 million religious Jews

Holy Places
Jerusalem, especially the Western Wall

Holy Books
The Torah

Holy Symbol
Seven-branched menorah (candle stand)

CHRISTIANITY
Founded
Around 30 CE, Jerusalem

Number of followers
Just under 2 000 million

Holy Places
Jerusalem and other sites associated with the life of Jesus

Holy Books
The Bible (Old and New Testaments)

Holy Symbol
Cross

HINDUISM
Founded
Developed gradually in prehistoric times

Number of followers
Around 750 million

Holy Places
River Ganges, especially at Varanasi (Benares). Several other places in India

Holy Books
Vedas, Upanishads, Mahabharata, Ramayana

Holy Symbol
Aum

SIKHISM
Founded Northwest India, 15th century CE

Number of followers 22.8 million

Holy Places
There are five important *takhts*, or seats of high authority: in Amritsar, Patna Sahib, Anandpur Sahib, Nanded, and Talwandi.

Sacred Scripture
The Guru Granth Sahib

Holy Symbol
The Khanda, the symbol of the Khalsa.

ISLAM
Founded
610 CE in Arabia (modern Saudi Arabia).

Number of followers
Over 1 000 million

Holy Places
Makkah and Madinah, in Saudi Arabia

Holy Books
The Qur'an

Holy Symbol
Crescent and star

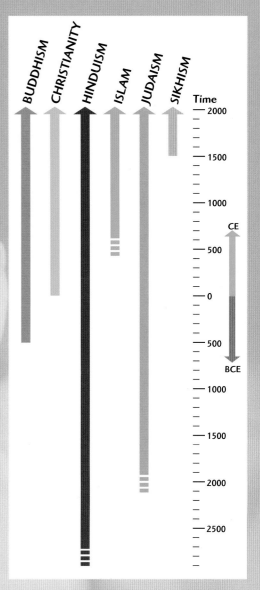

While some faiths can point to a definite time and person for their origin, others cannot. For example, Muslims teach that the beliefs of Islam predate Muhammad and go back to the beginning of the world. Hinduism apparently developed from several different prehistoric religious traditions.

GLOSSARY

Alms Offerings of food and other things, given to Buddhist monks.

Ascetic Someone who has chosen to live a life of strict discipline and self-denial for religious reasons.

Bhikkhu A Buddhist monk.

Bhikkuni A Buddhist nun.

Buddha Title given to Siddhartha, meaning "the enlightened one."

Dharma The teaching of the Buddha.

Dukkha Suffering.

Enlightenment A state of perfect understanding, in which a person sees things exactly as they are.

Karma (kamma) Actions that promote results after the event.

Koan A question to which there is no apparent logical answer, often used in Zen mental training.

Lama A senior teacher in the Tibetan Buddhist tradition.

Lay person Someone who has not been ordained as a monk or nun; an ordinary member of society.

Mahayana Buddhism The form of Buddhism that developed particularly in the Far East, and emphasized that it was suitable for all, not just for monks and nuns.

Mandala A special pattern, often made with colored sand, particularly at festival times.

Mantra Short phrases that people chant over and over.

Meditation Calming and training of the human mind.

Monastic life The life of monks and nuns, following the special rules that are known to Buddhists as the Vinaya.

Nirvana A state of peace, free from greed, hatred, and ignorance.

Pagoda A memorial containing relics of the Buddha or one of his followers, known originally as a stupa, it may also be called a *dagoba*, or a *chorten*. It may also be used for the whole temple complex, particularly in Burma.

Paramitars Qualities that Buddhists seek to cultivate.

Pilgrim Someone who travels to a holy place to express their commitment to their religion.

Poisons, the Three These are: greed, hatred, and ignorance.

Precepts Moral guidelines for following the Buddhist path.

Puja Worship; devotion to the Buddha.

Re-becoming The Buddhist teaching that people are always changing, depending on their karma. This is also believed to continue when one life ends, and then influences another which is about to start.

Refuge A place of security; Buddhists claim to go for refuge to the Buddha, his teachings, and his followers.

Reincarnation The popular idea in Indian religious thought that people have a soul that can pass from one body to another; this is often mistaken for Buddhist belief. (Buddhists believe that there is no permanent soul to pass on, but that lives influence one another through their karma.)

Retreat The opportunity to take time away from the routine of life for reflection and study.

Rupa An image of the Buddha, often used in worship.

Sadhu The traditional title for a holy man in India.

Samatha Meditation that leads to calmness of mind.

Samsara This world of constant change that we inhabit, influenced by greed, hatred, and ignorance.

Sangha The community of the Buddha's followers, both monastic and lay.

Scriptures Writings that are regarded as sacred to a particular religion, treated with respect, and used for guidance.

Shakyamuni (wise man of the Shakya clan.) A title for the historical Buddha.

Shrine A place of worship, having one or more Buddha images. It is sometimes the whole temple building, or a room used to house Buddha images.

Skilful means Knowing the right thing to do in a situation, without needing to follow rules.

Stupa A monument, containing the physical remains of the Buddha or one of his followers.

Sutra The name given to chapters of the Buddhist scriptures; it literally means "thread," because it gives the "thread" of a debate or argument.

Thanka A wall hanging, used especially in Tibetan Buddhism.

Theravada Buddhism The branch of Buddhism that developed in India and then spread through southeast Asia; probably the earliest of the existing forms of Buddhism.

Tulku A child who is believed to be born with the karma of a senior lama (popularly described as a reincarnation of that lama).

Vajrayana Buddhism The form of Buddhism found mainly in Tibet and the surrounding area.

Vinaya Rules for monks and nuns.

Vipassana Meditation leading to insight into the truth of life.

Wheel of Life Image which shows the Buddhist view of the constantly changing world, including the different realms of existence, and the links which illustrate how karma works.

Zen The Japanese word for meditation; a form of Buddhism based on meditation.

FURTHER INFORMATION

BOOKS TO READ

For comprehensive books on Buddhism, try:

Buddhism: the illustrated guide, ed. Kevin Trainer, Duncan Baird Publications, 2001

The Story of Buddhism, D.S. Lopez, Harper, San Francisco, 2001

Buddhism, Pushpesh Pant, Tiger Books International, London, 1997

Living Buddhism, Andrew Powell (with a foreword by the Dalai Lama), British Museum Press, 1989

Of the many school textbooks on Buddhism, two are by the author of this present book, and take the ideas that are outlined here further. They are:

The Buddhist Experience, Hodder & Stoughton, 2nd edition, 2000

Buddhism: a new approach, written with Steve Clarke, Hodder & Stoughton, 1996

The Buddhist Experience (Foundation Edition) Jan Thompson, Hodder & Stoughton, 2000, offers a simplified version of the main textbook.

The best-loved collection of the Buddha's teachings, and probably the oldest, is the Dhammapada (which translates as "the path of the teaching.") Its short sayings give a sense of the Buddha's teachings, and of the Buddhist way of life. It is available in many different translations.

Three adult books that are written in a very straightforward way, and give a good idea about the beliefs of modern Buddhists:

Teach Yourself: Buddhism, Clive Erricker, Hodder & Stoughton, 1995

Buddhism Without Beliefs, Stephen Batchelor, Bloomsbury, 1998. Offers a modern, relevant introduction to the Buddhist path.

The Miracle of Mindfulness, Thich Nhat Hanh , Rider, 1991, was originally written in 1976. It is a wonderful book for giving an idea of the way Buddhists train the mind to be aware of everything and to enjoy every moment.

Of the many books written by the Dalai Lama, try:

Ancient Wisdom, Modern World: Ethics for the New Millennium,
Little Brown & Co, 1999
General books that set Buddhism in context with other major world faiths:

What I Believe by Alan Brown and Andrew Langley,
Chapters/Transedition, 1999

Religions of the World by Elizabeth Breuilly, Joanne O'Brien, Martin Palmer, Facts on File, 1997

Festivals of the World by Elizabeth Breuilly, Joanne O'Brien, Martin Palmer, Checkmark Books, 2002

WEBSITES

www.buddhanet.net
This site gives a wonderful range of study materials from basic introductions to illustrations of Buddhist art. It covers all the main branches of Buddhism, and presents Buddhist teachings in an accessible way. It includes an online magazine, and teaching materials for all age groups.

www.manjushr.com
Visit this site for a list of Dharma centers in the U.S. and worldwide.

www.ciolek.com/WWWVL-Buddhism.html
This site keeps track of leading information facilities in the fields of Buddhism and Buddhist studies.

ORGANIZATIONS

Buddhist Association of the U.S.
2020, Route 301
Carmel,
NY 10512
This association publishes a journal and various programs .

Chicago Vajrayana Buddhist Center
1116 West Lake Street
Third Floor, Oak Park,
IL 60301
This center has branches in other states and offers classes and study programs.

Northwest Dharma Association
305 Harrison Street
Seattle,
WA 98109
Contact this association for lists of local groups which support Buddhist teachings.

Buddhist Churches of Canada National Headquarters
11786 Fentiman Place, Richmond BC
V7E 6M6
A link to all major Buddhist Churches across Canada. Also provides enquiry service about the traditions and customs of Buddhism.

INDEX